# Fierce Jobs
Storm Chasers
by Julie Murray

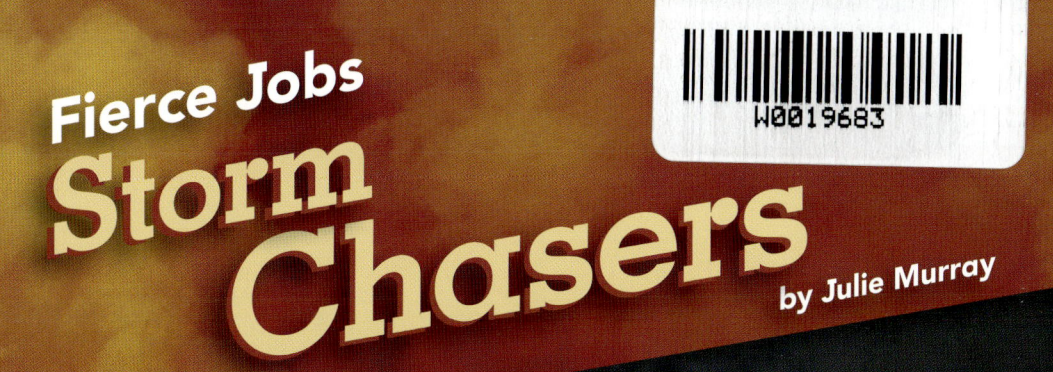

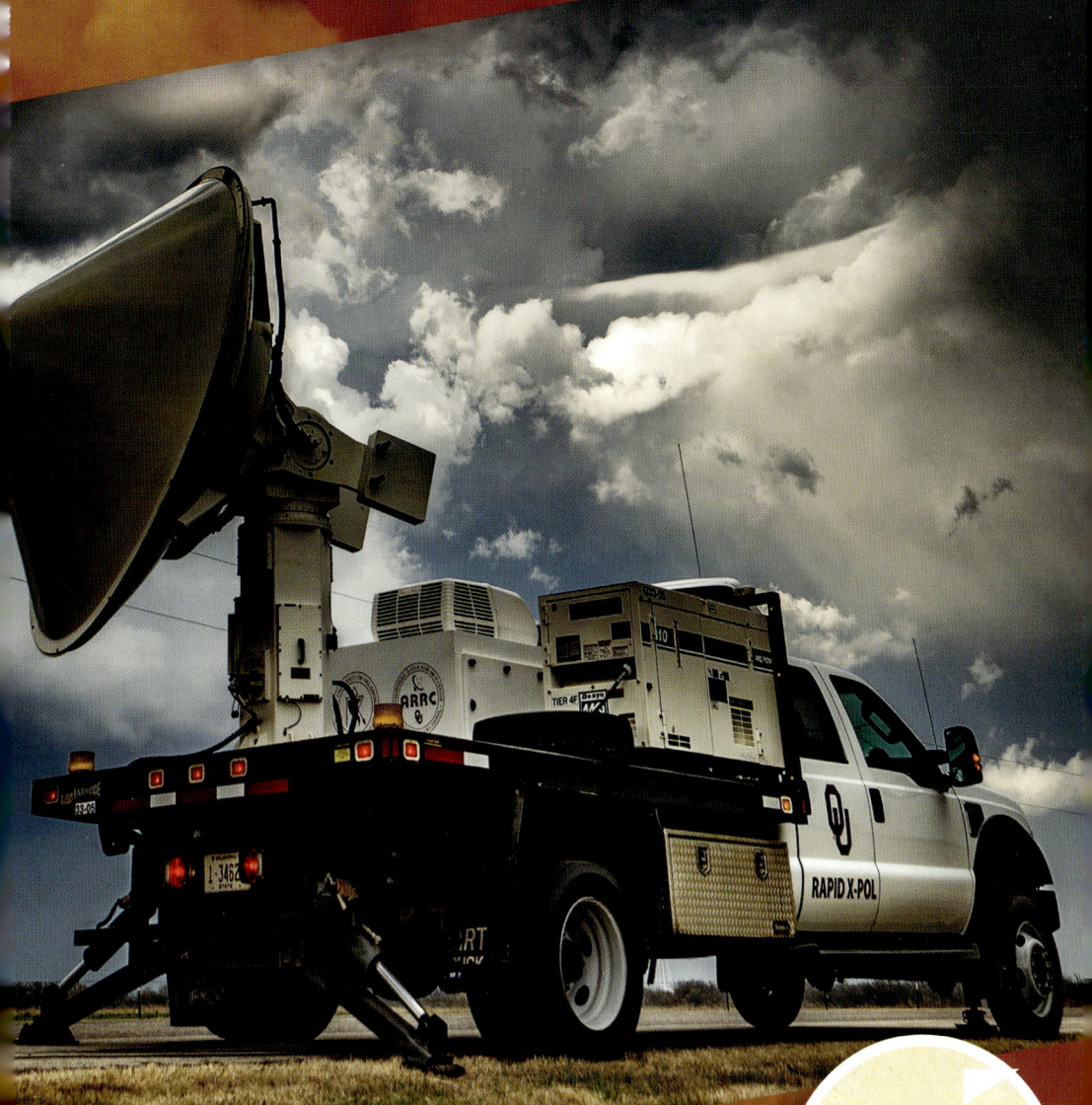

Dash!
LEVELED READERS
An Imprint of Abdo Zoom • abdobooks.com
2

Dash!
LEVELED READERS

Level 1 – Beginning
Short and simple sentences with familiar words or patterns for children who are beginning to understand how letters and sounds go together.

Level 2 – Emerging
Longer words and sentences with more complex language patterns for readers who are practicing common words and letter sounds.

Level 3 – Transitional
More developed language and vocabulary for readers who are becoming more independent.

THIS BOOK CONTAINS RECYCLED MATERIALS

abdobooks.com

Published by Abdo Zoom, a division of ABDO, PO Box 398166, Minneapolis, Minnesota 55439. Copyright © 2021 by Abdo Consulting Group, Inc. International copyrights reserved in all countries. No part of this book may be reproduced in any form without written permission from the publisher. Dash!™ is a trademark and logo of Abdo Zoom.

Printed in the United States of America, North Mankato, Minnesota.
052020
092020

Photo Credits: Alamy, iStock, Shutterstock
Production Contributors: Kenny Abdo, Jennie Forsberg, Grace Hansen, John Hansen
Design Contributors: Dorothy Toth, Neil Klinepier, Laura Graphenteen

Library of Congress Control Number: 2019956198

Publisher's Cataloging in Publication Data

Names: Murray, Julie, author.
Title: Storm chasers / by Julie Murray
Description: Minneapolis, Minnesota : Abdo Zoom, 2021 | Series: Fierce jobs | Includes online resources and index.
Identifiers: ISBN 9781098221126 (lib. bdg.) | ISBN 9781644944073 (pbk.) |
    ISBN 9781098222109 (ebook) | ISBN 9781098222598 (Read-to-Me ebook)
Subjects: LCSH: Storm chasers--Juvenile literature. | Tornadoes--Juvenile literature. | Severe storms--Juvenile literature. | Hazardous occupations--Juvenile literature. | Occupations--Juvenile literature.
Classification: DDC 551.553--dc23

Table of Contents

Storm Chasers 4

Equipment 10

More Facts 22

Glossary 23

Index 24

Online Resources 24

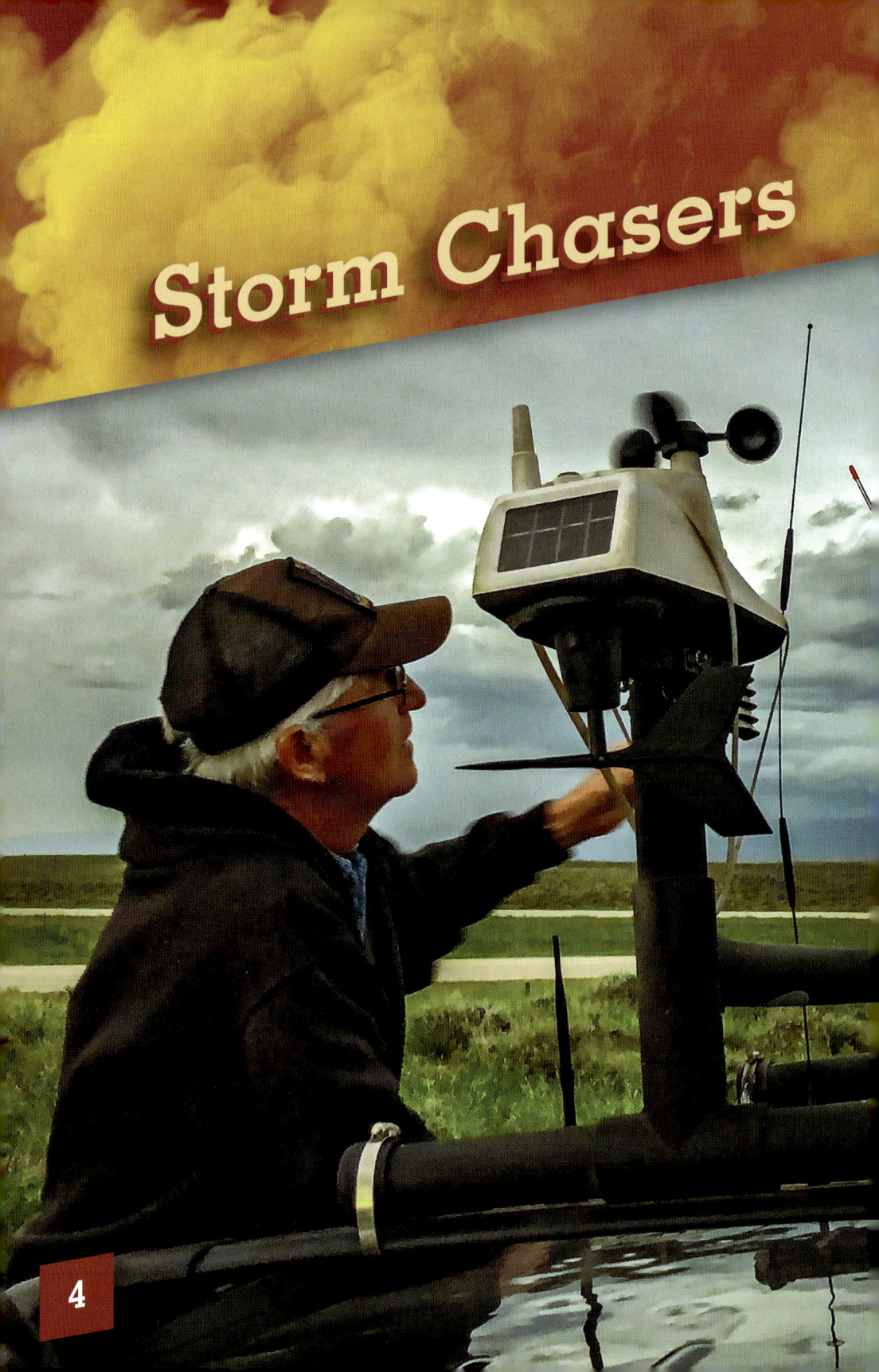

Storm Chasers

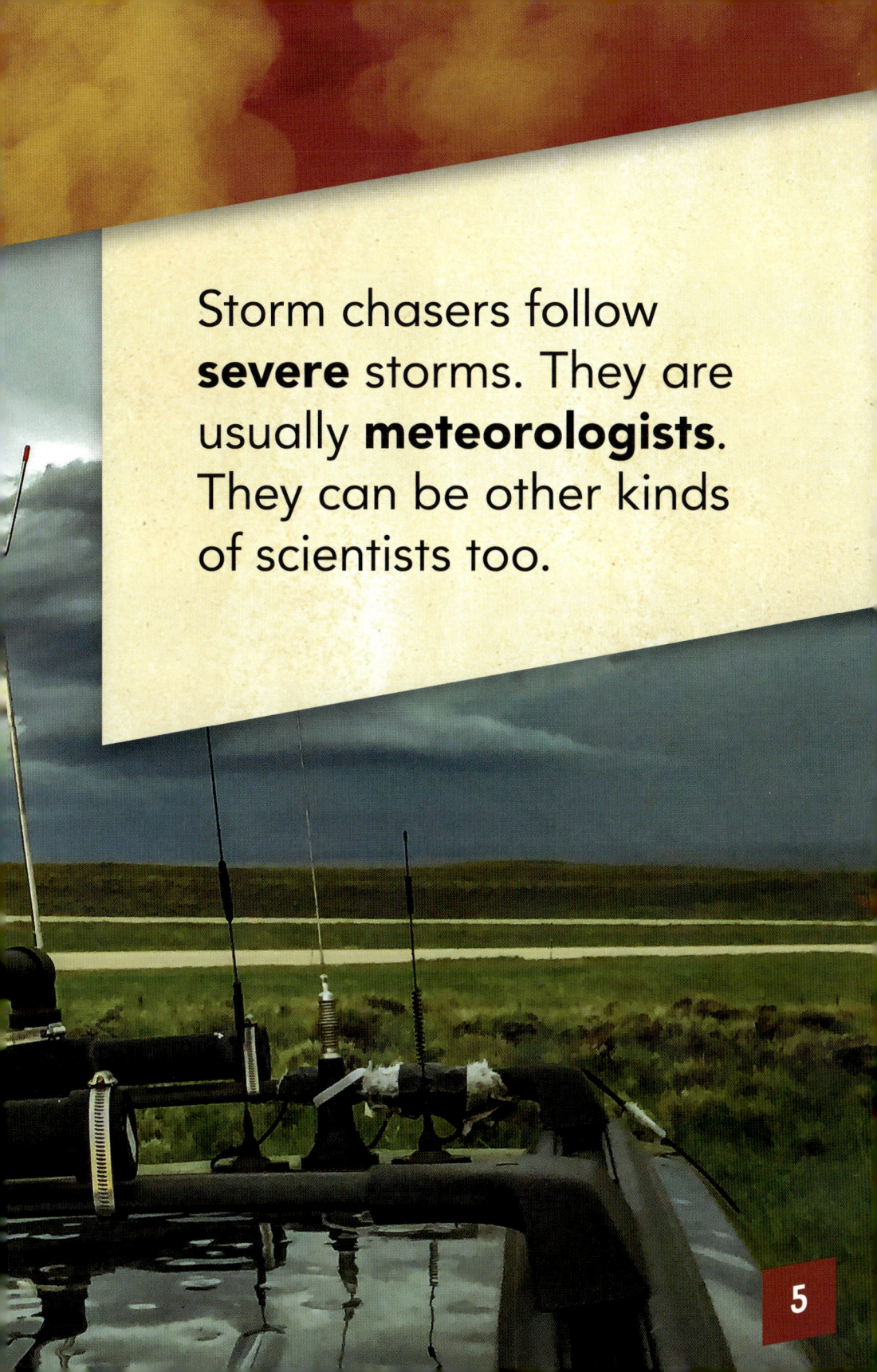

Storm chasers follow **severe** storms. They are usually **meteorologists**. They can be other kinds of scientists too.

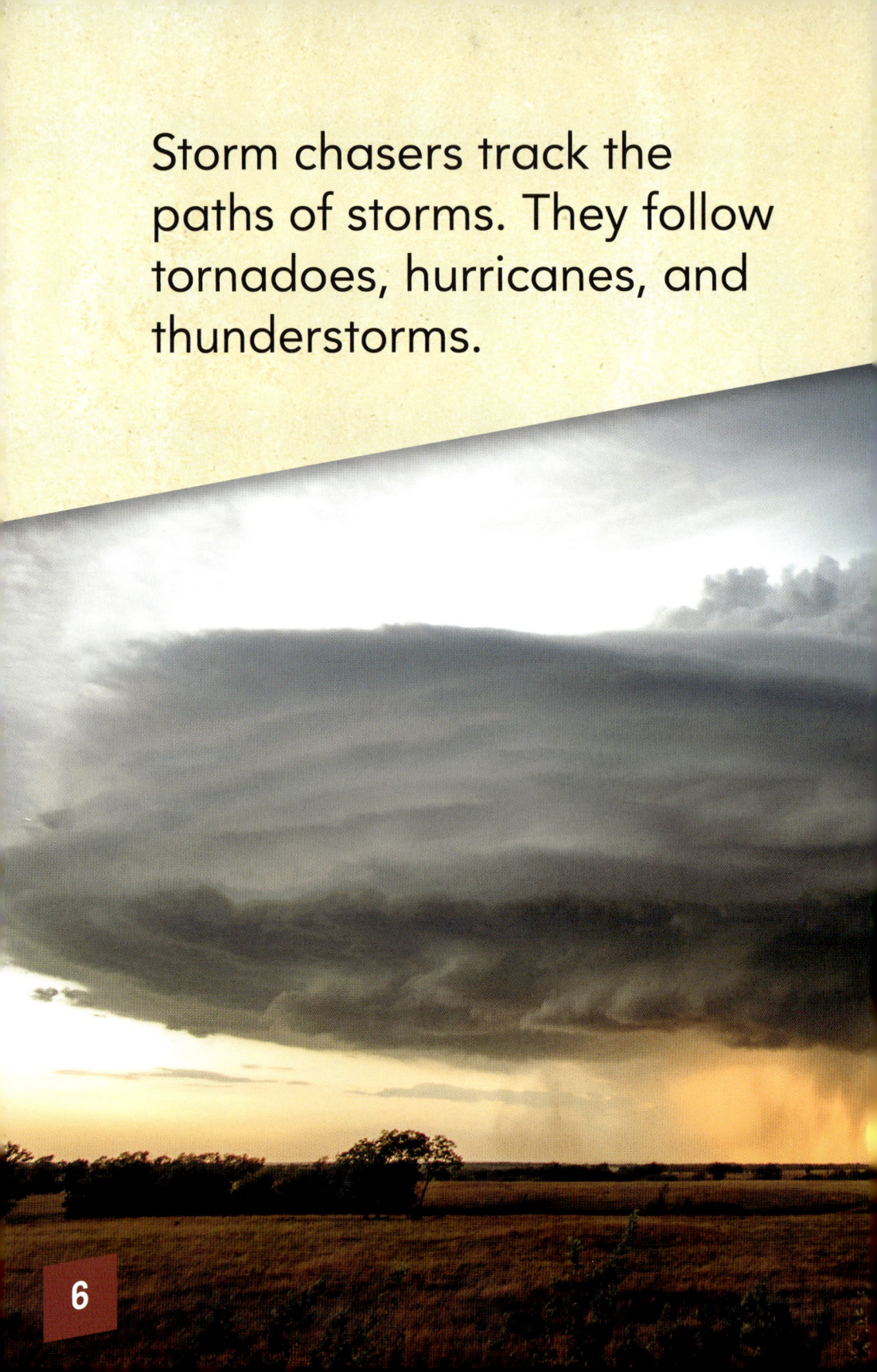

Storm chasers track the paths of storms. They follow tornadoes, hurricanes, and thunderstorms.

7

8

They may travel hundreds of miles a day. They gather **data** as the storm passes through.

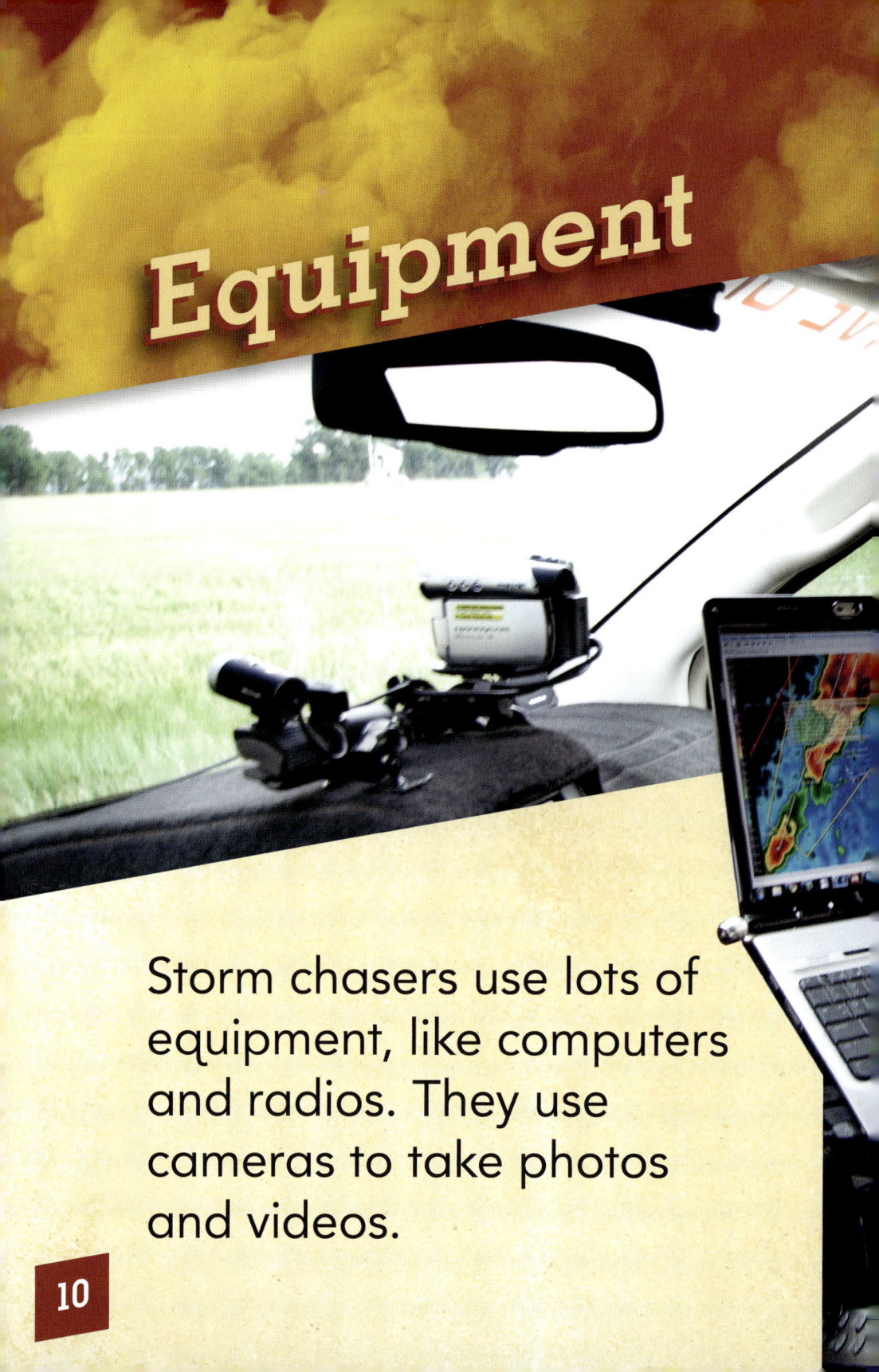

Equipment

Storm chasers use lots of equipment, like computers and radios. They use cameras to take photos and videos.

11

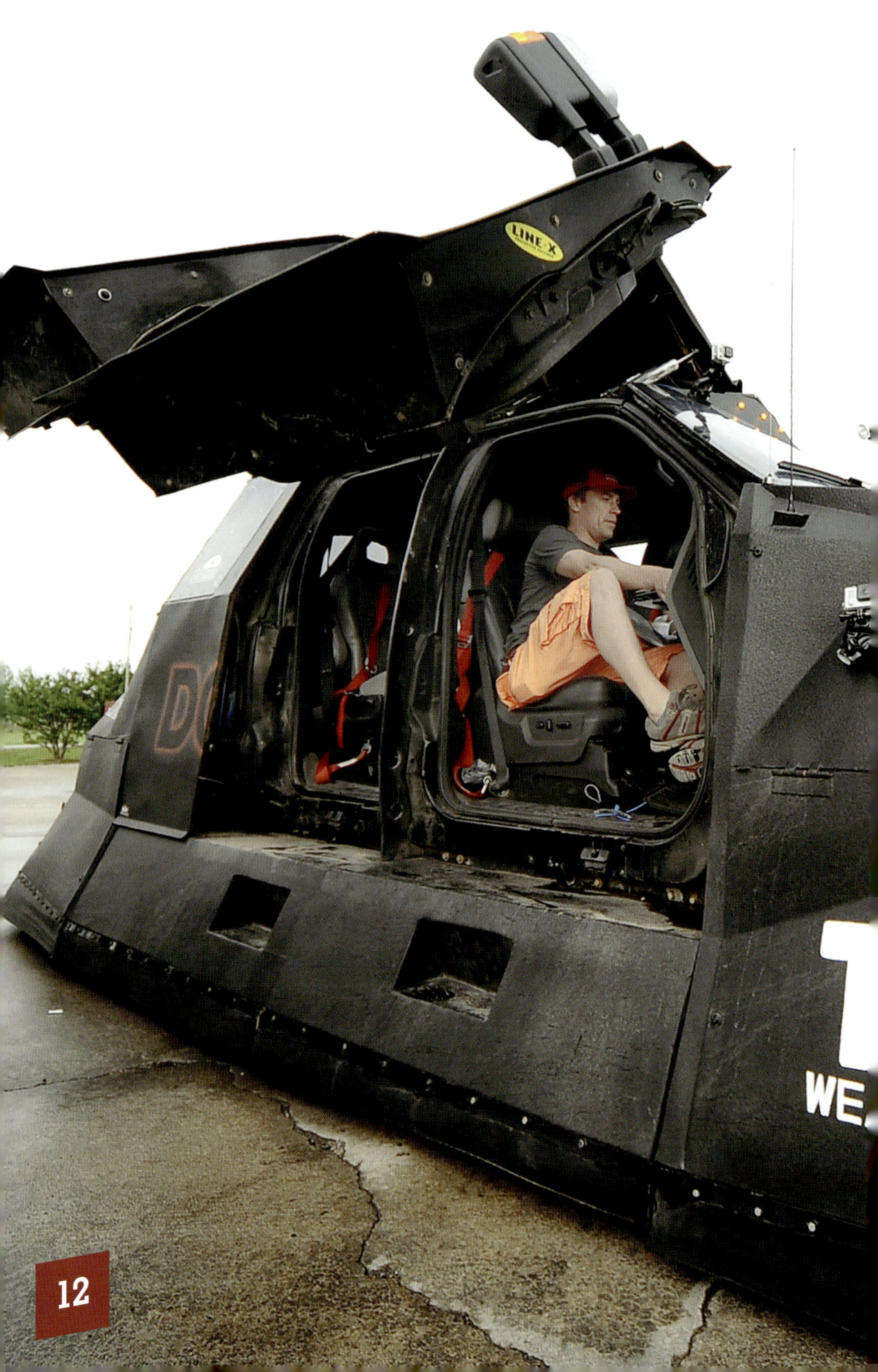
LINE-X

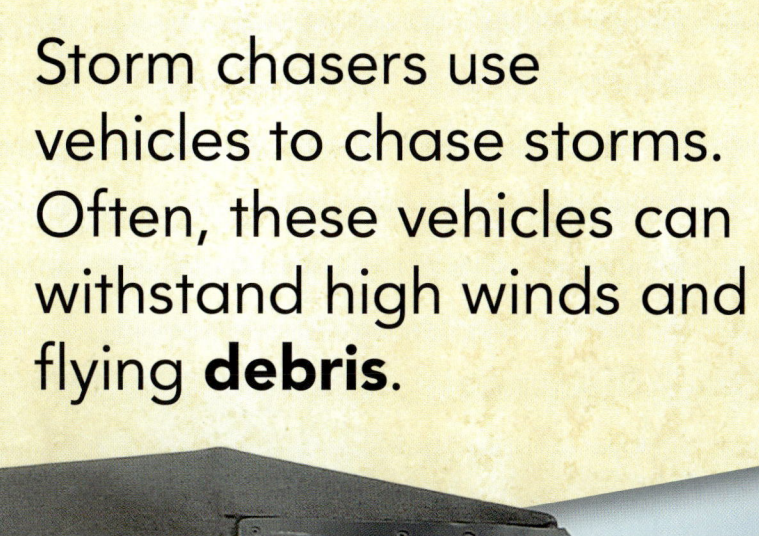

Storm chasers use vehicles to chase storms. Often, these vehicles can withstand high winds and flying **debris**.

A tornado pod is used to gather **data** from a twister. It is placed in the path of a tornado.

15

A **Doppler** on Wheels uses radio waves to collect information about the storm, like how far away it is and which way it's moving.

16

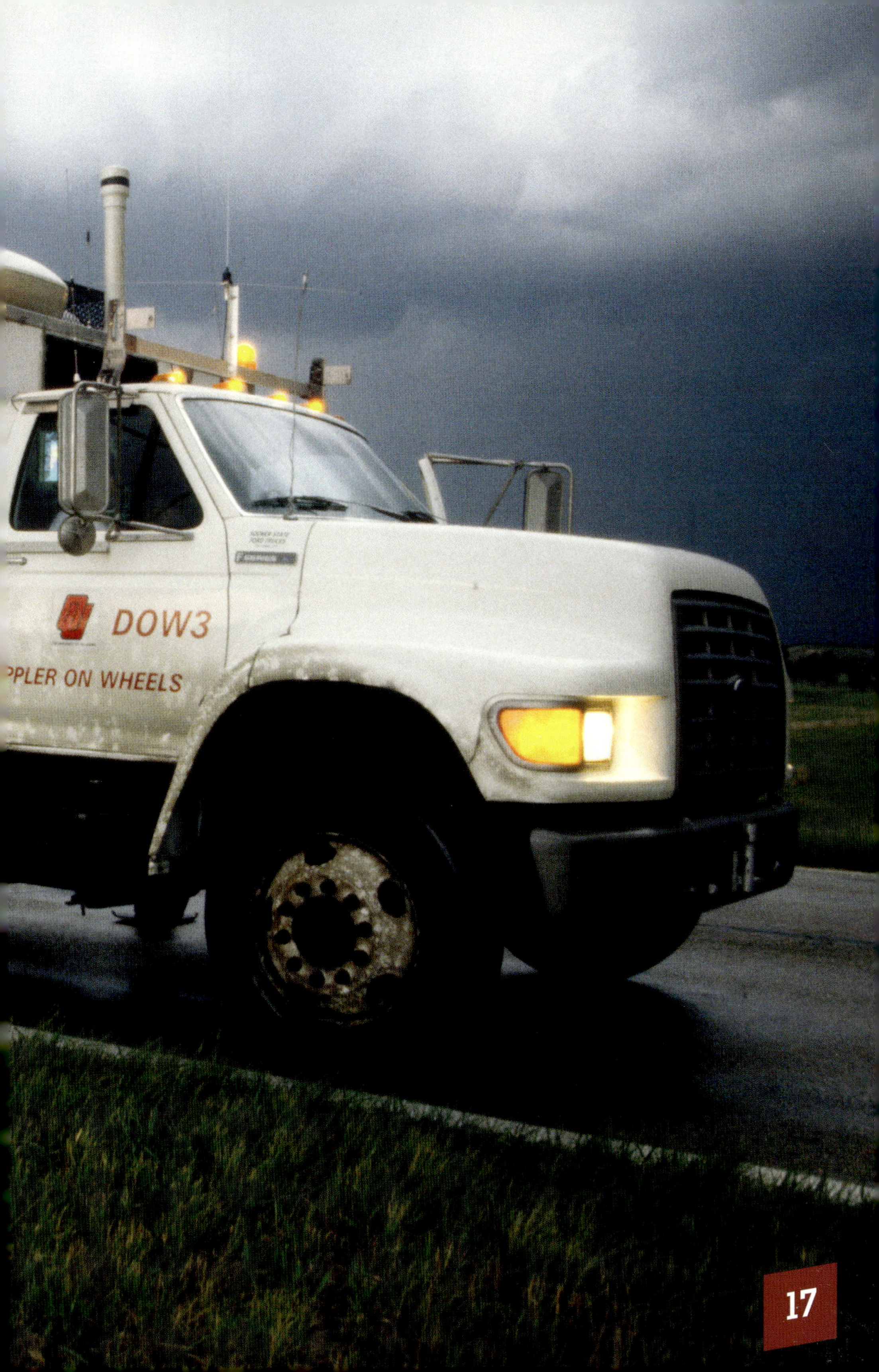
DOW3
PPLER ON WHEELS

Some storm chasers fly in airplanes. They fly right into the **eye** of a hurricane. They gather information about the storm.

19

Storm chasers risk their lives. Their work helps people better understand storms.

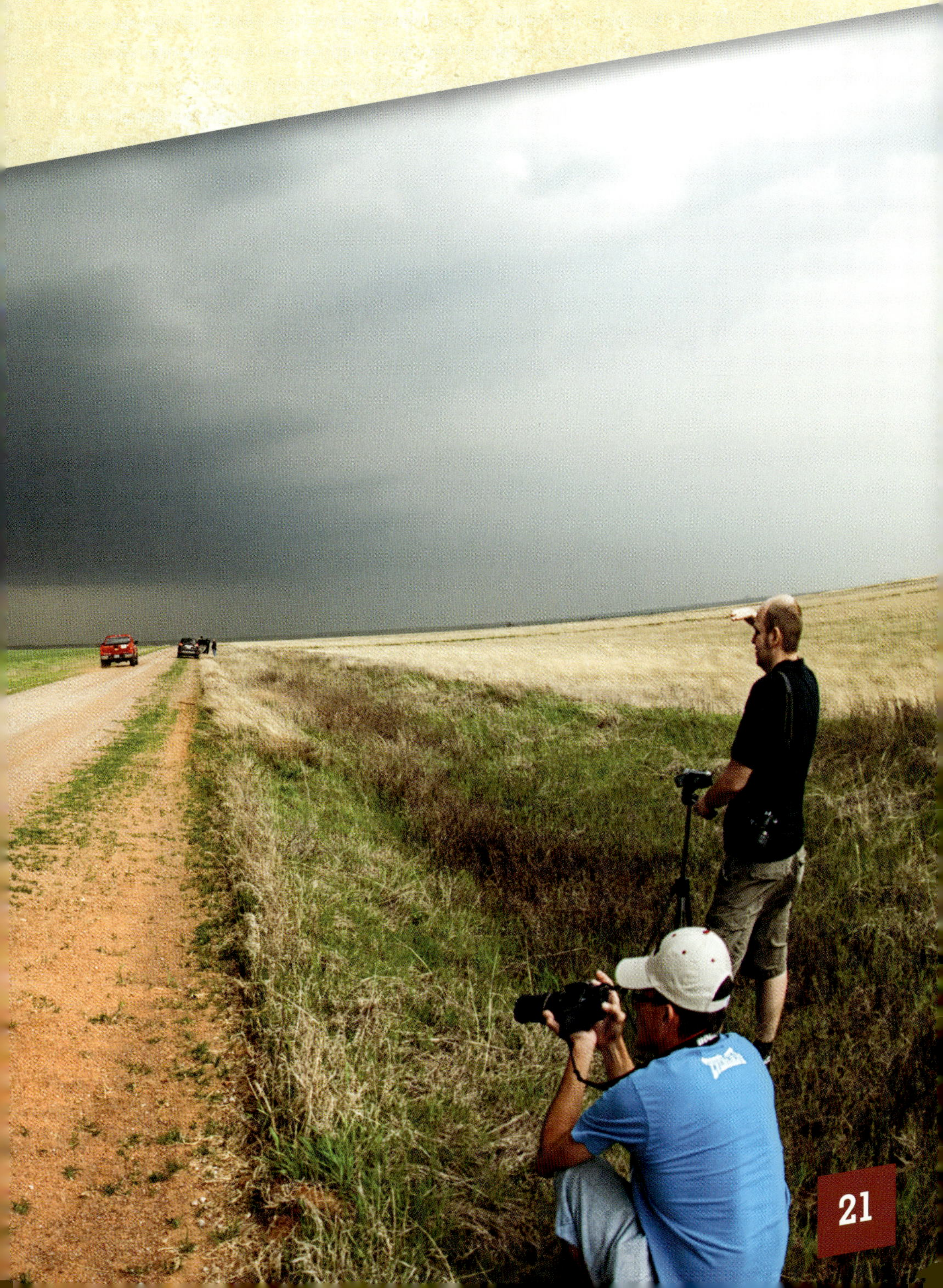

More Facts

- In 2013, three storm chasers tragically died. They were chasing a tornado in El Reno, Oklahoma.

- *Storm Chasers* was a TV show. It aired from 2007 to 2012. It showed the dangers and excitement that come with the job.

- There are more than 1,200 tornadoes that touch down in the US every year.

Glossary

data – facts, figures, or other pieces of information that can be used to learn about something.

debris – scattered pieces of something that has been destroyed.

Doppler – a radar tracking system using the Doppler effect to determine the location and velocity of a storm, clouds, precipitation, etc.

eye – the center of a storm.

meteorologist – a scientist that studies Earth's weather and atmosphere.

severe – very strong or intense.

Index

airplane 18

data 9, 14, 16, 18

Doppler 16

equipment 10, 14, 16

hurricane 6, 18

meteorologist 5

safety 13

scientists 5

thunderstorm 6

tornado 6, 14

vehicles 13, 16, 18

Online Resources

Booklinks
NONFICTION NETWORK
FREE! ONLINE NONFICTION RESOURCES

To learn more about storm chasers, please visit **abdobooklinks.com** or scan this QR code. These links are routinely monitored and updated to provide the most current information available.